The Ghostly Effect

Paul Surman

The Ghostly Effect
©Paul Surman

First Edition 2022

Paul Surman has asserted his authorship and given permission to
Dempsey & Windle for these poems to be published here.

Published by Dempsey & Windle under their VOLE imprint

15 Rosetrees
Guildford
Surrey
GU1 2HS
UK
01483 571164
dempseyandwindle.com

A catalogue record for this book is available from the British Library

British Library Cataloguing-in-Publication Data

ISBN: 978-1-913329-73-0

Printed and bound in the UK

for Anne Gerolemous

with gratitude for a long
and joyful friendship

Acknowledgements

Some of these poems, or versions of them, have previously been published in *Acumen*, *The Frogmore Papers*, and *The Journal.*

'Sanity' appeared in the Dempsey & Windle newsletter in August 2021.

'Still Life' was written for and performed at, a 'Poems in the Museum' event, at the Ashmolean Museum, Oxford.

I would like to acknowledge the advice and friendship of the members of Back Room Poets in Oxford.

Man is nothing else but what he purposes, he exists only in so far as he realises himself, he is therefore nothing else but the sum of his actions, nothing else but what his life is.

Jean Paul Sartre

Contents

THE GHOSTLY EFFECT

I want to believe in the reality
that hangs as a backdrop
to ecstasy or despair.

Wavering images of humans
float in puddles. In dark canals
at the end of rows

of boarded houses,
bright reflections of upended
shopping trolleys ripple

in murky water. We are only
the history of ourselves.
I examine the flow of minutes,

as if to verify I'm happening,
as time invents extraordinary
dragonflies and sunsets.

CONSCIOUS

I juggle precariously with my atoms,
calling it living, thinking that alive
is all about movement.

This me made from raw materials.
A life of energy and its echoes
in body and thought, breath

holding the mind aloft in an uncouth
paradise of memory and recognition,
an idea of blood heat and faint

electricity, that generates wild doubts
and confusion, but suggests
that being alive is meaning enough.

THE MIST

I stood very still
among the stark tree trunks,
against which a drifting mist
collided silently.

The dark outlines of trees
simplified everything. The mist
was time passing, eternity made visible.
I was softly transfixed,
I was trees and mist.

I was drifting away from myself
into the minimal wood,
into reality as a dream.
I was hushed into its quiet,
the appalling beauty of it—
bound to the blankness of mist,
as to the great amnesia.

My reason was numbed
by the implausibility of being
and not being. I mimed
a struggle to escape the moment,
and the trance broke.
Walking away through the trees
I was only the sound of my footsteps,
but that was enough.

THE PARISH

Returning from woods across fields of dew
our footsteps falter as we stumble over
the bare hoof-printed patch where cattle gather
and farm trailers rest in rank grass.

I imagine history limping along behind us,
a simple continuum of day—night—day,
watching us like the moon in a clear night sky,
or an owl on a fence post: unremitting stare.

For a moment it catches up. Past and present
overlap, hard to tell apart, except elm trees
appear again. A missing barn rebuilds itself.
The mind's ordinary magic explains it's night,

not morning now; even the air feels different.
I move silently, a ghost from the future,
and see that the frightened boy racing around
the barn's blind corner is my father.

TIME

I imagine it as the sonorous tick of an old clock
in an empty room,
>>in an empty house,
>>>>in an empty street,
where nothing of significance happens.

Perhaps the owners of the house are all dead,
or on holiday. Birds fly by, quick as seconds.
Rain on the overgrown pond disturbs its peace.
A postman with capacious bag over his shoulder,
walks up the garden path, pushes a single letter
through the letterbox, and walks casually away.
He may return again tomorrow, or he may not.
We cannot know his thoughts.

>>>>>>Briefly it is noon.
Then the afternoon slumps into a listless evening,
evening into night. Time's ordinary procession.
We cannot know its thoughts, we are its thoughts.

SANITY

is an undemonstrative madness,
a tidy precision. Like standing in clean clothes,
accounted for, and smugly well adjusted.
Sanity tries not to be obsessive, but sometimes
likes to feel like well-polished shoes.

You can't be sure of anything in a life story,
where birth and death are the front and back covers
of a book that's still being written.

There's some logic to things, sanity imagines,
but worries it might get things wrong,
that it's using an erroneous alphabet, or an incorrect
set of numbers. But yes, the mind likes to think
it knows its own dimensions, to kid itself
it makes some kind of sense.

SHADOWS

Not the light and shade of those summers past,
or dappled shadow moving in the breeze
like someone breathing, for day after day
of birdsong and peace. Not any chiaroscuro,
no matter how delicately etched. I remember
our dissatisfaction with relentless ease,
a disquiet we kept to ourselves.

I do not think of such pale examples now,
but of deeper shadows, those close relatives
and secret agents of the night
who are in uneasy league with daylight,
and play one off against the other
in order to exist. The kind of shadows
that, lacking a conscience, might conceal anything.

SIRENS

elbow their way through city streets,
making an average civil peace
seem like pious contemplation.

People wince like priests besieged by sin,
as if pursued by hooded riders
astride engines of apocalypse.

In the mind's maddened eye
cracks appear in pavements, glass shatters,
tall buildings tremble near collapse.

But when the noise has ceased,
its shock-wave passing down another street,
everything is reversed.

That which was broken apart by sound
is whole again, glass restored
to window frames, buildings solid and still.

We are surprisingly elated in the aftermath.
But a solitary nerve still screams
pestilence and harm. It always will.

EVOKED
for Christine

I imagine you
on a warm summer evening in the garden.
A sudden fragrance, the breath
of a flower.

         Retracing your steps,
it has disappeared, but is still more real
than its vanishing. If it was a sound
it would be inaudible, if a thought
unspoken.

         It is tangible as the space
between withheld and expressed,
between darkness and light,
remembering and forgetting.

While you try to recapture its fragility,
waiting in silence for its return,
every garden in the world holds its breath.

UNKNOWN

Who she was,
and where she came from,
nobody knew.
Only that they saw her,
in the afternoon heat,
many years ago.

She had walked down
the sloping path,
next to the red brick wall
covered in magnolia,
past flower borders,
the cypress, the cedar,
classical urns and sundial,
a huddle of dark pines.

Past where the spray
from the ornamental fountain
had darkened the path,
and shepherdess, nymphs
and satyr gestured
from stone plinths.

She was lost to sight
near the ruined church,
and was never seen again.

Gardeners straightened up
from what they were doing
as she went on her way.
They would never forget her
but couldn't explain why.
She looked old-fashioned
they said, and was smiling.

AT TATE MODERN

A tall man in a long grey gaberdine coat,
and wide-brimmed light grey hat,
plain grey trousers and soft black shoes.

He appeared to float through the galleries,
and as he walked his coat flared around him
in a bell shape, but he made no sound.

I saw his face, but can't tell you about it,
or his eyes. If I had to guess, I'd say
he must have come from nowhere at all.

He was not so much a person as like one.
His colour was the same drab shade
as worry, and I don't think he smiled.

On his back he carried a deflated rucksack
that looked as if it had nothing in it.
I guessed his pockets were empty too.

He was going somewhere: nobody dared
stand in his way. I don't know who he was,
but feel certain he was an artist, or a poet.

THE ART OF BEING ALIVE

is seeing things and knowing what you see.
It can take a lifetime to master complex skills,
but seeing what's in front of you, and knowing it,
is the difficult thing. Lady's Mantle

growing out of a crack in a collapsing wall
is easy to pass by. Trees painting a house front
with splashes of fluid shadow. A gate
hanging lopsided as a bird's broken wing.

Time's message displayed on a church tower,
or on the grey certainties of public buildings,
is of no significance if glanced at quickly.
Even the faded brilliance of a daytime moon

is a beauty too silent to be paid attention to
in a wilderness of things too obvious to see.

LIT WINDOWS

Lights are on in other people's houses,
where they live their other people's lives.
I observe this curtained luminosity,
to which our local night holds close.

Ghostly gardens, a vixen's scream,
horses restless in enigmatic fields
surround the future and the present.

But beyond the edge of darkness
people live in a world of light
and movement. I imagine lives like ideas.
I imagine factories and bus stops,
conversations and silence,
day's bleak expressionless windows.

By day I wait for darkness,
craving the silent beauty of lit windows.
Later I wait for sleep to lead me
into the wilderness of my mind,
to make the dreams that are its poems.

LIFE SPEAKS

Bells chime, crows caw, leaves shush,
and I am the only question there is.
The crows said that, not me. I love crows,
that sound they make, so grimly alive.
Their voices cannot help telling the truth.

Time passes, wants you to speak for it.
You say nothing. There is no such thing
as time, but I tell you, this useful figment
will be the death of you. Time passes
and all things are eventually changed.

Look! See those woods on the hill opposite.
They cast a fringe of jagged shadow
where time passes but remains, and silence
waits forever. That's me sitting with them.
Where are you if you are not with us?

Now I can see you, walking that rutted lane.
A red kite soars over you, tips sideways
on its wings, looks down, and sees
a puny human. That's you, only half alive,
shambling through your starving thoughts.

You think I might be merciful, and I might.
But know this, I don't give a damn about you.
What is it you're thinking? Do you think
the devil has cloven hooves and God wears
golden slippers? Are you a fool among fools?

Bells have chimed, leaves have whispered,
crows have spoken, shadows are cast,
and I, Life itself, have called you a fool.
What did you expect? What is it you want?
I say, love me for what I am, or not at all.

O CROW

pecking at the carcase of the field,
just so's you know,
I'm watching you.

I'm not dapper like you are,
but my eyesight's good,
and I'm stealthy. Don't ignore me
just because I'm softly spoken.
With all day at my disposal,
I'm watching you.

I might get my binoculars
to see your sleekest detail.
Don't say you haven't been told,
I've got my eye on you.

When you sit hump-backed
in a tree, watching me,
I'm watching you, and be warned,
the dark at the back of my mind
is darker than your sinister
stare, your funereal coat.

You are a corvid, but I
am human, and humans laid waste
to a planet. Know this:
some might think you are bad,
with your love of a corpse,
but I'm far worse, and I'm
looking straight at you right now.

ESSENCE

Not the parson's words that echo off stone,
saying something that cannot be traced
to its source,

a message carried through time
like a casket of bones, or a sliver of wood,
that crumbles in thought

to subtle theologies of shadow and dust,
the weight of the church
afloat on a dream of its meaning.

Not reverence for the sounds of prayer
that decay past the range of our hearing,
or the promise of light

in the secular dark at the edge of the village,
where the road turns back, and a lane
goes deep into woods. Not any of these.

Imperfect I return to where I fade
from the light, to find my way by touch
along the dangerous softness of the night.

ORDINARY BEAUTY

The day rests in its afterthoughts.
A Tesco delivery van parked opposite,
indicator light winking aimlessly,
has an abandoned feel to its ungainly presence.

A cat sidles from here to somewhere else.
The air, hardly breathing, makes itself ready
for sleep. I am standing, hands in pockets,
looking at the hedge I cut earlier, pleased
with my efforts.

                        How full of potential
the empty road feels, set free from its burden
of traffic, in a local stillness
that feels universal, this hesitation
before night returns with natural dignity
to its task of staring at eternity.

THE OWL INCIDENT

In the shade of the lane late one summer afternoon,
years ago, I remember a little owl, its gaze wide-open
as a field. Since when, quiet as its flight feathers,
the moment has flown from memory.

I want to return to those owl-infused coordinates,
the bird their only certainty, but all there is
is a mind-etched forgery, under a sky that might belong
to myth or legend. All that remains is owl.

The village's day was, I imagine, as ordinary as any other.
A mechanic in the garage finishing off a car, rubbing
greasy hands on grimy overalls. Someone in the post office
buying stamps. The parish in all its simplicity.

Time moves slowly as the shadows of trees, and the past,
sealed inside the mind, is far-distant as a god.

AN OLD MAN GOES TO SEA AGAIN

He sits in his cottage
facing the prow of the dark,
dreaming the winds of the century,
sailing the solid ship of his house
into the lift and thud of the night
through backyard gardens
towards the open fields.
Weathered by memories
he goes on alone as oceans slide
an undertow beneath his thoughts
and trail the lives of the dead in his wake.

He sails the pitch and toss and troughs
of the ditches and ploughs on
through the plumes of trees
towards the distant glow of the city
in which he will never arrive.
Some nights he forgets to batten the gate
so that it swings and crashes
in a storm too great
to venture the decks to shut it
and the trees sing close
with the hiss of the sea.

SUMMONING GHOSTS

A smile.
First sight of the sea in years.
The hat she used to shade her eyes.
Stillness and heat of a summer afternoon.
A moment's instability, stepping from riverbank to boat.
Someone knocking softly on the door of an empty house.
A drift of smoke from a woodsman's fire.
Laughter in a garden.
The passage of stars.

STILL LIFE

A red drift veined in the marble table top,
the plump lustre of those grapes.
Studied inflorescence in a vase,
that knife not carelessly laid down.

The spiralled curl of half-peeled fruit
placed purposely to test the painter's art,
the drop of water that bulges inside
its surface tension. They are not the story.

After the artists obsessive precision,
long hours of patient lingering over details,
they are merely a collection of surfaces,
shine and sheen, transparency and glint.

But painted objects lend weight to the mind
as if they or thought could be grasped.

BREATH

I lie awake thinking of air,
the here, there and everywhere of it
adrift in familiar village streets,
dreamlessly asleep in woods.

I imagine soiled historical air.
Lascivious air that clings close
to the body of someone's lover
—closer than they ever could—
at the same time as it loiters
aimlessly at the edge of space.

I think of how the idea of heaven
seems airless to me. How the air
is as large as planetary weather,
and tiny as the breath of a bird.

COAST

Waves obsessed with the power of repetition
grasp at a shoreline they can't hold on to.
On land, a nest of mastheads leans against the sky,
angles jumbled. Life above the tideline:

cuttlebone, sea kale, s*urfers against sewage,*
the cool domestic interiors of an expensive dignity,
blackbirds doing a late-evening dance
of sudden rushes and sideways tilts of the head

on even-tempered lawns, but behind the easy
smoothness a shattered sea continues, a wreckage
of motion, and rampant agility, the difficult beauty
of cause and effect over which gulls develop

a troubled conversation, and tonight the moon's
lamp hangs, looking as if it's been snapped in half.

DESERTED MEDIEVAL VILLAGES

They are hinted at by crop marks.
Outlines of old walls hidden
under new growth, whole villages,
history once alive with people

who were aware of the sunlight
on their skin, the coolness of water,
and night settling in more quickly
as days edged towards winter.

Whose thoughts could slip free
of the harsh routine of labour,
to be easily snared by love,
or wonder at mist rising off fields.

Who feared God and dreaded illness,
knowing that life itself is godless
but beautiful at times. Like a song
stumbling blindly over fallen walls.

LIFE GOES ON

Hot

Real abandoned frontier towns soon become
film sets of abandoned towns.

Warm winds are stand-in ghosts
that make floorboards creak, hinges rasp,

summon hot dust to spiral up itself—
an empty phantom that, boneless,

flops to the ground and writhes ecstatically
in badly acted death throes.

Cold

We still build temporary homes,
subject to unpredictable abandonment.

A hut in Antarctica, its shelves
stocked with cans of long-forgotten food.

Extreme cold sits at its bare benches,
a glacial ghost making invisible notes

in frozen air that is brittle as labels on the tins.
It hunches over itself in mock existence.

SENSITIVITY

You said you could tell the thickness
and weight of snow on a roof
merely by sitting under it, would know
exactly when it altered state
from white to whatever colour
water is. An ecstatic thaw.

There was, for sure, no holding you back
or letting you go. I must have dreamt
or been confused into thinking your moods
controlled the phases of the moon,
that you could see the stars by daylight.
They were all quite mad of course

those other men, to say you could travel
in more than one dimension at a time,
knowing simultaneously, for example,
lava-flow and ice. Love was impossible
with so much uncanny interference.
I know you can hear me think of you again.

MIDWINTER

You can hear the cold tightening the frost
until it gives way, leaving a raw silence
that hardens to a standstill in your flesh,

where blood slows to a chill acceptance.
You are too far into the weather to turn back.
The certainties of science are like a clash

of shadows and all your subtleties are really
superstitions. Consciousness is what you
cling to, even in this deteriorating season

you believe it is gifted because it feels so
real. You tell this to yourself and to the tree
outside your window, you have grown to love.

AT NIGHT I LISTEN TO THE ROAD

listening quietly to itself, obsessively practising
its fixed idea of perfection. There is nothing
more pleased with itself
than a road contemplating its paradox,
the way it comes and goes and remains.

It disturbs with its constant flowing past,
but part the curtains, and it's still staring back
at the street light's vacant gaze. Later, headlights
break and enter your bedroom, swerve and fade
into the mystery of someone else's life.

SUBTERRANEAN

Sleep is an underworld where we are myth.
Here too we live barely credible lives, same
as in daylight where we are slowly interred
under moments that try to be lucid as dreams.

We travel daily between waking and sleeping,
along the familiar road of ambush. Surrender
our passport, which the border guard stamps
with a glance. Our life is a working hypothesis.

Dreams come from an interior, where we trudge
through dripping cave systems of imaginings,
whose rushlight reality illuminates from within
the depths of living under skies of thought.

THE LIGHT

stares back at me as I close our bedroom curtains.
Embedded in the dark opposing hillside,
its shine goes beyond a useful purpose, feels
as if it pleads with me to answer its urgent request.

Porch light of isolated house, or solitary illumination
of a dirt-deep farmyard, whose desolate outlines
were abandoned there by nightfall,
it's settled down to be the one bright thing.

The night's cold haunts my thoughts
as they stagger towards its persistent signal, beamed
from whatever outpost it belongs to. It feels
like the light that shines behind mind's shadow.

I imagine its gleam settling like snowfall on the fur
of a passing fox, who's stopped to consider a landscape
that is neither now nor here, but another time and place,
where a light burns at the edge of a valley of myths.

I AM A MYTH

Images flow into my head through wide-open eyes
to become the grandeur and ruins of what I've seen.
Are fugitive as soon as they cross the glassy emptiness
of seeing, and slip out of sight into border lands,
soon to be lost inside mind's cramped vision of infinity.

They appear later in the half-light of a fading memory,
or step, naked and drug-bright, from the fever of a dream.

They had been kept captive in the drab unreality
of cognitive back streets. Blackened red-brick terraces
where yellow light from corner shops is alchemic
on the leaden surfaces of roads that lead nowhere.

In continuous darkness, under the irregular shine
of synaptic stars, I know that everything is conditional,
and awkwardly relative, in the fiction of who I am.

LEGENDARY

We were born to havoc. A man's world
of sweat and threat, a time of complicated,
aggressive dreams.

The landscape was parched, all boulders,
plants that lived on next to nothing,
and dried-up river beds. The pure blue skies
were perfect for the flight of scavengers,
we wore their dizzying shadows
over our heads with pride.

The towns were dusty and given to disquiet.
It was best not to look comrades in the eye,
the polished weaponry of a glance could slash you.

Our dangerous leaders thrilled us.
Always new populations to conquer,
whose simple subsistence
we garlanded with hardship.
But despite all this, some of us survived
and lived to a great age,
or even worse, fell in love.

SINBAD DROWNING

Under the weight of my weightlessness,
I descend a steep and swirling sea
to splintered wrecks, and the crushed
ghosts of those already drowned.

I am a cargo of ill at ease, awkwardness,
and false starts, yet haunted by the turn
and turn about of shimmering shoals
I quickly turn into sunken treasure.

Where sea-monsters might pick me
ragged to the bones, I drift to an insensate
standstill, becoming softly embedded
in the undersea, where I should drown.

But I breathe in oceans and survive.
Water's voices—light and clear, or a groan
of its heavy load—sing to the distant call
of the moon's unsteady transformations.

Whatever it is that life beneath the surface
is working to expose, the water's pressure
propels me back, swaddled in bubbles,
full of conversations with the deep.

ATLANTIS

Wealthy householders try to decipher
a tumult of cries and agile conversation
rising from the street. They fear the hubbub
of faceless people, but bear lightly
the ferocity of light and heat. Outside
shadows stride across uneven walls.

The poor, who know so much more
than the rich, will not lead them
towards the safety of a ramshackle freedom
in the chaos of overcrowded alleys.

The King and Queen—heavily crowned,
and overdressed with power—are compelled
to dream the myths that made them.
They wake with a shout, walled up in the palace's
gaudy imaginings, where they spoil their sons,
who see only minor strategies
in their mind's gold mirror.

Pale exalted daughters read poems aloud,
struggle with dilapidated meaning,
and slowly starve, as time is measured
in forebodings that their lives
will never be real enough to last,
that disaster comes slowly from within.

DUMBSTRUCK

The mad lurch along the street,
the brave stride fearlessly, and louts
swagger, shouting out loud
their holy fear. I am separate.

I am talking silently to thought,
which has its own life to live,
staring eyeless into infinity.

It reads from a glossy catalogue
of the possible. Finds a boat on a lake,
tiny waves slapping at its sides.

Dips a hand in the water, pulls out
a bright blue fish from behind
the enigmatic grey-green veil.

The fish flounders and gasps
in its despair, there but hardly alive
in thought's private reality.

When thought seeks out mineral, root,
or star, it finds them all. Whatever
thought wants it gets away with.

It looks around, tries to to delve into
the history of soil, discovers ants,
a tangible land crawling with detail
under the phantom sky.

MY DREAM ENDED

without beginning. I don't remember
arriving at the chain hotel, its long
dark corridors, silence bleeding
from anonymous rooms, hotel staff
speaking to me telepathically,
saying my reservation was invalid,
for subtle reasons I accepted
without dissent, then left.

Looking again, the hotel was a nuclear plant,
implacable mind of monolithic drabness.
In the vast car park huge loudspeakers,
trumpet-shaped flowers on thin black stalks,
blared their anxious thoughts, or mine.

Walking uphill in sunshine, past abandoned
half-built buildings, a fawn-coloured owl
was standing on the air inches from me.
The passers-by took no notice. Then the owl,
staring at me, became a lifeless deer's head.

THE ROAD

The road's moods of moonlight
and rain, ice and summer heat,
lull us into acquiescence.

Awake, my mind drifts through walls,
comes to rest, languid at the road's edge.
All traffic has ceased, and the road
breathes as if alive. As for me, I am not
a dream, or a ghost. I am thought.

Mind moves along the road, looks
at hedges and houses, listens to
a silence dark as night's animal.

Then it sees the truth, as simple
and always there, as weather.
Knows there is only one road,
a branching, creeping form;
shapeless creature from the deep past,
that shambled from ancient way
to sunken footpath, to bridleway;
from lane, farm track, and animal route
to tarmac's nerveless technology.
An agent of conveyance, uncertain
as my ghostly road of thought.

ENTANGLEMENT

Somewhere inside my thoughts
I am coming in from the rain.

A detective at a desk in my mind
stays there long after everyone else
has gone. He's obsessively playing,
over and over, indistinct CCTV
of someone who might be me
coming in from the rain.

He looks for something
he can't pin down. Some detail
others failed to see, difference
between innocence or guilt.

Watches me come in from the rain,
a shadow among shadows, as time
flows by like an androgynous god.

I'm asleep at an unspecified address
in sleep's reality, a mediocre room,
beyond which an unfamiliar street
drenched in rain, is held in the gaze
of tall disinterested street lamps.

I'm tormented by an image of me
continually coming in from the rain,
believe my mind is coming to arrest me.
I wait for its car to pull up. Footsteps,
a knock on the door, denouement.

SADNESS IN INFINITY

Beauty is a familiar landscape repeated
somewhere else, the same green slopes,
the tree almost correctly positioned,
everything so nearly right it hurts.

The clock reaches the appointed hour,
a significance it will repeat. We made
elaborate machinery for it, lavishing
exquisite care on its lovely dials.

We arrange to meet by the town clock,
or visit the white-coated doctor
down the passage of time, where he
waits for us with his amiable smile.

While we falter, time never stumbles.
We loiter next to the terrible sadness
of trees, their deep sighs of inaudible
exhalation, that time casually accepts.

At night we might dream in symbols—
clouds, or wild animals—hallucinatory
flesh on mind's deepest abstractions,
directed at the mystery of awake.

ASPERGER'S DIAGNOSIS AT SEVENTY

The previously invisible now startlingly evident.
I didn't know my destiny from birth had been
to go on this quest, slaying countless common dragons.
Nobody thanked me, they didn't seem to know
they were there, or how terrifying they are.
Always they expect scales, horns, fire breathing.

I only half-understood that I had to find my way
through austere labyrinths, performing impossible tasks.
An entire life spent clinging comically to cliff faces,
over sheer, gut-wrenching drops, or wrestling
improbable mythical beasts with magical powers
and eyes that could vaporize with a glance.
At least, that's what it felt like.

Perhaps I should have guessed what it really was,
but I didn't know. Those adventures I've mentioned
are metaphorical of course, the only kind
I'm almost adept at. If I should appear ill at ease,
or say something odd, just give me a moment
to finish fighting a monster in another dimension.
I always win in the end. You go on, I'll catch you up.

PLANTSWOMAN
for Christine

To converse with plants you must speak silence,
an idiom whose manuscript is air and peace,
impervious to all the claims of scholarship,
a language of purest quietude.

I have often seen you walk the garden
from flower to flower; touching, watering,
tending to each plant, and though I am not fluent
in this language without words, I have listened to you
and everything you have said makes perfect sense.

AUTUMN WALK

Grim's ditch -
prehistoric earthworks
near Nuffield village - Chilterns

The trees are tall guardians,
but cannot intervene, their leaves
slow-burn is sombre in the mist.

In a field, a breed of black sheep
are dark outlines: crows
stalk the spaces between them.

Other crows scrape the sky raw
with their sound; cold air touches us
with a prehistoric hand.

I know we are intruders,
that we are the real phantoms
in any imagined landscape.

My mind prattles nervously
in an ancient language
of bone, antler, and flint.

The sky brightening unexpectedly,
is a revenants' sign, saying:
stranger, be on your way.

I stumble down the gully's fissure,
pushed and shoved
by my own erratic progress.

We stop where there are no crows,
only a small opening of sunlight
in the austere ecology of silence.

TONIGHT

What there is of the world other than the cleverness
of electricity, or the finite mysteries of plum trees—
I do not know. Night commences its transformations

and I imagine a blank-faced x or y, much like me,
strolling across a suburban lawn that's already
becoming somewhere else, yet to be determined.

Where once there were flower beds, there's nothing
he can recognise. Only an absence of geranium and iris,
potentilla, rosemary and lavender. The privet hedge

is already missing in the undergrowth of the world.
He looks up at the stars, his face so expressionless
it's as if he's not there. What he knows of tranquillity

or believes things mean, is unknown to me. I see him
gazing into the spaciousness beyond the stars.

TWO-SPEED AUTUMN

Life speeds up around me while slowness gathers
like clouds in my limbs. When the postman arrives
carrying his bag of earthly gifts, it seems as if he walks
as fast as Charlie Chaplin. Today, somewhere, apples
may be falling quick as rain from orchard trees.
Each apple-thud part of a dull rumble of ripeness.

My thoughts are slow as ever. Intense black dots—
small birds—stream across the sky like low-level jets.
The hours escaping go too fast for clocks,
but I am so still and quiet I can hear the woods
change colour fifteen miles away in the Chilterns.
Beauty everywhere as I start my long slow stumble.

THE UNCERTAINTY PRINCIPLE

We thought we owned the earth,
but when we parcelled it out
we lost its meaning:
meadows, scrubland, solitary tree,
poppies, old man's beard.

The sky had no say in the matter,
having forgotten itself
while attempting to round up
stray clouds that drifted
through long invisible fingers

Erudite surveyors travelled
all over lost territory, looking for it.
Going wherever they imagined
they were meant to be going,
to measure outlines of the land.

I imagine them in heavy tweeds
or stiff oiled-cotton jackets,
against changeable weather;
looking much like one another,
or anyone else, but trundling
measuring wheels, and carrying
tripods and theodolites.

Afterwards, one surveyor,
with a faraway look on his face,
would remember a telephone box
next to a road sign, where a young
woman crossed the road, holding
a pink umbrella in the drizzling rain.

NOTHING

There was a nothing in the crowded dark
of the woods. It was there the murder happened.
The body wore a blank expression that told
detectives nothing. Nothing was ever proven.

There were clues, but nothing was one step ahead.
You could sense it looking over your shoulder,
but on turning to see, it was never there. A nothing
of no fixed abode. Suspicion fell on a pale nothing

that loitered on street corners at all times of day,
doing nothing. Hands in pockets: gaze everywhere.
Even a nothing that hid in columns of figures,
living under the pseudonym of zero, was suspect.

We know so much about nothing, but now it lives
beyond our jurisdiction, in near perfect vacuums
in regions of space where atoms are metres apart:
absolute nothing so pure it might almost be a god.

WAR

In early evening from the A-road
the mountains seem under attack, as if
raked and strafed from unseen positions.
The clouds piled up suggest explosions,

billowing of dust and smoke. I think
of a shell's trajectory always ending
when its maker's inscription is blown apart.
Then I wonder what will survive

in the yellow water of the loch;
in the pine forest's acres of lichened bark;
of the paths in the daytime heat; bilberry
and juniper, the delicate fruiting of moss.

Later, the street light is a bright incendiary,
everywhere is strewn with the debris of rain.

THE GODDESS AND THE OAK

The statue of the goddess
has wide-open eyes, bright and lifeless as the moon,
that focus on what we cannot see:
her homeland in unreal landscapes
where shapes of the invisible are said to exist,
and she is unobtainable, even to herself.

Such beauty is not for the living, her symmetry
draws you towards a sinister perfection,
will place your mind beyond reach.

Turn away from the dangerous absolute of purity,
the impossible soon becomes cruel;
walk instead in the ambivalence of the earth's
imperfect landscape, the living and the death of it,
its eternal infancy and old age, growth and decay.

Like the goddess it will not grieve for you,
but you may lie down with it, under an oak tree's
irregular arms, its scars where branches are missing,
the life and damage of it, and feel you are almost loved.
You might imagine you belong there, that you are as real
as the hopeful myth of who you think you are.

BANG

"But no one was there to see it."
Steve Weinburg in *The First Three Minutes*

You know how it is in those dreams,
when I opened my mouth to gasp
everything went in reverse, I breathed out
not in, a sudden explosive burst
and with it came the sun and terrified
populations of the earth: all I could do
was watch. I list here just some of what I saw
starting at no particular place
with umbrellas, suburbs, species, rain.

Out of the darkness of my gaping mouth
came murderers, string, and visions
of the virgin: then beauty—nothing
just beautiful, but beauty itself.
On and on things hurtled
and among it all a universe of useful things
we keep in kitchen drawers, and books;
books by Wittgenstein and Schopenhauer
and Kant turning over and over in my
outgoing breath; and history, all of history
happening at once with everything
so close together that Genghis Khan
and Attila the Hun mingled with Hegel
and Marx; and for a moment, just
for a moment, I thought they would
work something out for the good.

Then mattresses, mammoths, tigers, cigars,
nothing was sacred, nothing made sense,
Pandora's box—as yet unopened—Mozart
just mad about Constanze's arse;
then toffee and tea and dreams about falling,

tickets, troubadours and trees
and random accidental special effects;
atoms and harbours, wood nymphs
and satyrs, pianos and sofas and things
whose purpose I never could guess;
menhirs and tubas, lions and lapwings,
prophets and seers, charlatans and shamans,
gurus of business or sexual excess;
Christ and Krishna, Buddha, Mohammed,
making it all up to try and explain,
but getting it wrong, or never quite right,
as popes and priests, disciples and mullahs,
followed and feted, muddled, distorted them
over and over and over again.
Then ranches, robots, electrical disturbances,
distortions of space and of time, zeppelins,
volcanoes and underground trains;
vortices, solstices, samovars, sin; camels
and Arabian bands. I was becoming exhausted
by the breathing of objects, people
and concepts, continents, languages,
digital data, radio frequencies
and as I breathed, between
all the knowledge, events and alignments,
a darkness was pouring, growing
and spreading, outwards and onwards
until blackness obscured all of infinity's space;
and still the inventory expanded:
with plasma and portents, junk yards
and herons, sailcloth and cycles,
linnets, barns, electric guitars;
mazes and bookends, barbers and llamas,
concertinas and ley lines, complex and bloody

medieval wars, industrial progress
and laughing hyenas, plainsong ascending
into ancient stone roofs and out-of-love
lovers on long French weekends.

Slowly the blackness engulfed all about me,
my breath and the things its progress brought forth
become nebulous and distant, a celestial darkness,
full of galaxies, universe, planets and stars,
far exhalations in which I lost interest
though they sparkled like gems,
made from those things on the madness of breath,
those things I had breathed to life in creation
waiting for me to breathe them back in.

IN THE WOODS

A squall frightened the deer
from parkland into these woods,
where they knew the trees
would look the other way,
and keep their secret.

When they stand still
the deer are like a memory
of them being here. They are volatile
like this, as if they only imagine
they exist. More spirit than real,
they are always ready to slip through
a gap in their breathing and disappear.

I wonder if they hear our thoughts
hesitate at the edge of who we are

WINTER CEREMONY

Before it starts, I might be thinking of
electricity or the Milky Way. I flick
the light switch: the observance begins.

I put yesterday's dry crockery away
—and knives, spoons and forks—
with care not to drop or break anything.
I lay the table for our breakfast,
then open the curtains.

I move at a measured pace.
One moment, the next, and the next,
are questions and explanations.

It's dark, but I feel sure the sky
still exists. My face stays solemn,
but thoughts smile at this.
I wonder whether life is a poem,
or a poem is life, and vow
to try to solve that problem later.

I pour my orange juice,
take a sip. Open the kitchen door,
and stand in the chilly doorway
to listen to the birds sing.
They confirm the sky is still there.

I say good morning to the birds,
out of politeness, and with thanks.
Then go slowly, but with quiet purpose,
to finish yesterdays poem, or begin today's.
For a moment life is as simple as this.

If you have enjoyed *The Ghostly Effect,* you may also like
Seasons of Damage and Beauty (2021)

Paul Surman

Seasons
of Damage
and Beauty

Available from dempseyandwindle.com
and to order from bookshops
ISBN 978-1-913329-40-2

Reviews of *Seasons of Damage and Beauty*

"This is a poetry of question and reassurance. Beauty resides in small moments of disturbance. There are poems that mark the passage of time and the inevitability of death. Many poems here explore the hinterlands of sleep and wakefulness, imagined worlds and imagined states of being.

Surman doesn't believe in magic, but he is no stranger to magical thinking. He invests "a vast invisibility" with the power to scratch graffiti into the sky amidst birdsong and the quiet business of lives being lived.

A pure and gentle curiosity underpins much of this work."

— **Pat Winslow**

"Paul Surman's new collection settles at the crossroads between landscape and mindscape. Surman witnesses and bears witness to birds, squirrels -- all the small things to whom the land really belongs—with a keen eye and keener affection. His greatest miracle is a blackbird's song, or a murmuration. He also ponders the imponderables. Night, self, philosophy, light — the poet wanders through them, muses, sits quietly, aware that he is neither more nor less than he is, another animal. An assured, beautiful collection."

— **Jennifer A. McGowan**